I
342.73   Evans, J   472-92
Eva   Edward

Freedom of the press

DATE DUE

Freedom of the Press

Freedom of the Press

J. Edward Evans

 Lerner Publications Company · Minneapolis

Front cover photograph by Greg Helgeson

Cover illustration courtesy of the Library of Congress

Library of Congress Cataloging-in-Publication Data

Evans, J. Edward.
     Freedom of the press in the United States / J. Edward Evans.
         p.   cm.
     Includes bibliographical references.
     Summary: Explains what freedom of the press is, its history in
colonial times, its meaning in the Constitution, and current
controversial issues challenging the boundaries of this freedom.
     ISBN 0-8225-1752-3 (lib. bdg.)
     1. Freedom of the press—United States—Juvenile literature.
2. Press law—United States—Juvenile literature. [1. Freedom of
the press. 2. Press law.] I. Title.
KF4774.Z9A27   1990
342.73′0853—dc20
[347.302853]   89-13297
                                                               CIP
                                                               AC

Manufactured in the United States of America

1 2 3 4 5 6 7 8 9 10 99 98 97 96 95 94 93 92 91 90

Contents

Determining the limits of freedom of the press can be difficult. Television, for example, is a powerful medium that can influence young people. Who should decide what can be shown on TV?

1
The Free Press: Freedom of Information

Of all the rights that United States citizens enjoy, which are the most important to a free society? Freedom of speech? Freedom of religion? Freedom to vote for the candidate of your choice?

Freedom of the press might not rank first on many people's lists. It may seem as though this freedom directly affects only the small group of people who publish newspapers. Viewed that way, the freedom of the press clause in the Constitution is little more than an insurance policy to make the business of journalism less troublesome.

Freedom of the press, though, is not about protecting a select group of people in a business venture. It is concerned with protecting all the people of the United States. Freedom of the press really means freedom of information. That is why the term "press" refers not just to newspapers, but to other organized methods of spreading news, such as radio and television broadcasts, books, and motion pictures.

Freedom of information guarantees the right of every citizen to know what the government is doing. A free press provides people with the facts they need to make intelligent decisions about their country. It helps them to be valuable members of society by keeping them abreast of current ideas and issues.

Without a free press, a democratic form of government would be unlikely. Only ideas approved by those in

7

power would be published. Without a free press, government officials could violate other rights, such as freedom of speech, religion, and assembly, with little fear of being stopped.

A free press is the watchdog that guards all of our individual freedoms. That is one of the reasons why freedom of the press is among the rights protected by the First Amendment to the Constitution. The First Amendment states that:

> Congress shall make no law respecting an establishment of religion, or prohibiting the free exercise thereof; or abridging the freedom of speech, or of the press; or the right of the people peaceably to assemble, and to petition the Government for a redress of grievances.

Thomas Jefferson, third president of the United States, felt strongly about the importance of a free press:

> The people are the only censors of their governors. . . . The basis of our government being the opinion of the people, the very first object should be to keep that right (full information of government affairs) and were it left to me to decide whether we should have a government without newspapers or newspapers without a government, I should not hesitate a moment to prefer the latter!

Thomas Jefferson, third president of the United States, championed freedom of the press, but later tried to limit that freedom for his political opponents.

Support for an entirely free press has never been unanimous in the United States, however. At times the media seem to cross the bounds of fairness or decency. Should a magazine be allowed to print lies? Should a book be allowed to ruin someone's reputation? Should television, which exerts a powerful influence over young people, be allowed to show any program it chooses? Must the government sit back idly when a newspaper spills secrets that are vital to the national security? Should society put limits on pornographic films?

Questions such as these have forced many people to debate the limits of freedom of the press. What is to be done when the press acts irresponsibly? Even Thomas Jefferson, a champion of freedom of the press, had little tolerance for newspapers that printed what he thought was malicious criticism. In 1803, while president, Jefferson wrote, "I have...long thought that a few prosecutions of the most prominent offenders would have a wholesome effect in restoring the integrity of the press."

Every society must decide how to deal with the abuses of the press. In the United States, the government sets mosts of the controls. But if

In a society that values freedom of the press, journalists are free to question and criticize the government and other powerful institutions.

the government controls the press, then it also controls the information citizens receive. That is exactly what the United States' founders hoped to prevent.

The answers to questions concerning a free press are not always simple. The Constitution and the Bill of Rights were adopted to ensure freedom for the people from abuses of government. But exactly what did the writers of the Constitution mean by freedom of the press? Does the Constitution give us freedom to print anything, no matter how irresponsible, or does it simply mean freedom from **censorship**? (Censorship refers to the act of withholding, confiscating, or deleting material so that it cannot be printed, broadcast, or distributed.)

Even if everyone agreed on what the writers of those documents meant, many questions would remain unanswered. The founders could not have predicted all the situations or cultural changes in later centuries. The issues concerning freedom of the press must be continually studied and debated to prevent important rights from being taken for granted.

Each generation must struggle with the questions of freedom, responsibility, and security. The lessons of the past must be studied; the influences

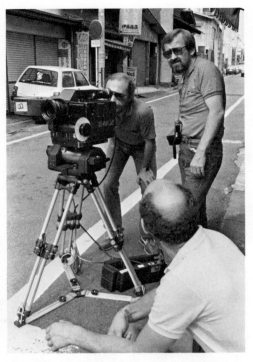

A moviemaker is guaranteed freedom of the press by the First Amendment, just as is a newspaper writer. Freedom of the press extends to all forms of media, including movies, radio, television, books, and newspapers.

of the present must be identified. Only by understanding the lessons of the past and being aware of the problems of the present can we make sure that the flow of information in the United States remains free.

2
The Origins of the Press

The right of individuals to freely express opinions has been proposed and debated for many centuries. As early as the fifth century B.C., the Greek playwright Euripides wrote, "This is true liberty when free-born men, having to advise the public, may speak free."

Before 1459 most information was spread by one person telling another. The kind of detailed information or complex thought that could best be expressed in books or pamphlets was not available to the average person. Such writings had to be hand-copied, a costly, tedious process.

In 1459, however, Johann Gutenberg of Germany developed the printing press. His process used movable type and allowed many

A reproduction of the first page of the Bible that Johann Gutenberg printed

copies of a manuscript to be made in a short period of time. For the first time in history, ideas and information could be spread quickly and accurately.

William Caxton recognized the value of Gutenberg's invention. In 1476 he set up England's first printing press. Through Caxton's press, English people were introduced to many foreign books, which Caxton translated before printing. The printer also reproduced Old English literature that he translated into the language as it was spoken in his time. His work was financed by noblemen and supported by the king.

Early Battles for Control of the Presses

Although some officials focused on the advantages of the printing press, many more viewed the new

William Caxton, the first English printer, shows his printed material to King Edward IV. Caxton used his new press to print classic works of literature.

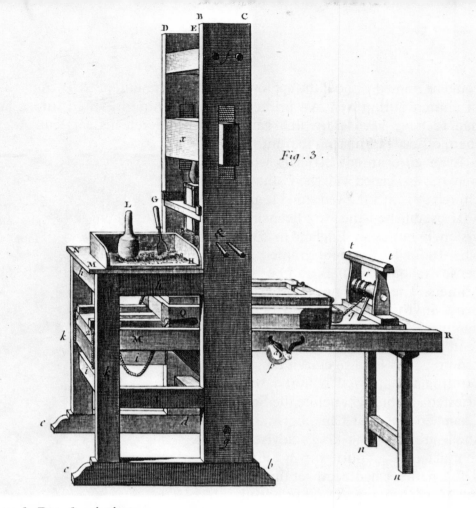

An early French printing press

invention with alarm. Many people believed that any idea that did not agree with the official government or the church was a threat to society. Before the printing press was built, it had been relatively easy to stop the spread of these ideas. But with this new method of printing, people had access to radical, uncensored opinions.

During the early 16th century, more people began to criticize some of the policies of the Roman Catholic church. Using the new press, the critics carried their ideas rapidly from one community to another. Church officials moved quickly to stamp out the threat. A short time after Gutenberg introduced his press, the Catholic church ruled that nothing could be printed without the approval of church authorities. All printers had to have **licenses**, which gave them official permission to print.

Even government officials who were not associated with the Catholic church quickly followed suit. Henry VIII established the first licensing system in Protestant England in 1530. The Tudor government granted licenses to only a small number of printers. They were not allowed to print anything until it had been approved by an official censor.

In the late 16th and early 17th centuries, any English citizen caught printing unapproved material was arrested and brought before the **Star Chamber**. The Star Chamber was a small group of the king's advisers that acted as a court with no jury. The Chamber had been set up as a means of bringing to trial powerful people. Eventually, however, the Star Chamber became a special weapon used against the king's enemies.

The Star Chamber punished anyone who offended the king even remotely. In 1632, for example, a lawyer named William Prynne published a book that was critical of the theater. King Charles I and his queen enjoyed the theater, though, so the book was considered an attack on the royal couple. The Star

Chamber sentenced Prynne to life imprisonment, fined him a large sum, ordered his ears cut off, and

Charles I became king of England in 1625, when he was 25 years old. He tried to silence his critics by sending them before the Star Chamber. Charles I was beheaded in 1649.

burned all copies of the book they could find.

Despite the threat of such severe punishment, secret printing presses kept turning out material. Seventeenth-century England was flooded with unsigned pamphlets in which people expressed their views on many forbidden subjects. Slowly, the persistence of the secret presses paid off. In 1641 the English Parliament abolished the Star Chamber.

Some writers continued to plead for an end to government control of information—an end to government licensing of printing presses. In 1644 John Milton published a pamphlet, called *Areopagitica*, without a license. In his passionate plea for a free press, Milton wrote, "Let [Truth] and falsehood grapple; who ever knew Truth put to the Worse, in a free and open encounter?"

Half a century later, in 1694, censorship by licensing was finally ended in England.

Birth of Newspapers

The forbidden pamphlets of the early 17th century frequently sparked far more interest than the officially approved writings. As an increasing amount of thought-provoking reading material became available, many English people wanted to learn to read. The greater number of readers, in turn, increased the demand for more reading material.

As England became a world power and its influence spread across the seas, its citizens took a great interest in world affairs. Demand for news increased so much that three men were inspired to publish the first weekly newsbook in 1621. Called a *coranto*, the publication contained translated items from the news-sheets of Europe.

This coranto and the imitations that followed it did not survive for long. In 1632 the English government suppressed all corantos. It was not until the abolishment of the Star Chamber nine years later that weekly newspapers reappeared. After licensing restrictions were lifted, news began to flow more freely than ever before. In 1702 England's first daily newspaper, the *Daily Courant*, was started.

By its very existence, a thriving press promoted the cause of freedom. For the first time, people did not have to depend upon the government to tell them what was right or true. Freedom of information was slowly being loosed from the grip of a select group of authorities.

AREOPAGITICA; 9

A

SPEECH

OF

Mr. JOHN MILTON

For the Liberty of VNLICENC'D PRINTING,

To the PARLAMENT of ENGLAND.

Τὸ λδ᾽θερον δ᾽ ἐκεῖνο, εἴ τις θέλη πόλε
Χρηςὸν τι βάλαμ᾽ εἰς μέσον φέρειν, ἔχων.
Καὶ ταῦθ᾽ ὁ χρήζων, λαμπρὸς ἐδ᾽, ὁ μὴ θέλων,
Σιγᾷ, τί τάτων ἐςιν ἰσαίτερον πόλε;
Euripid. Hicetid.

Ex Dono Authoris

This is true Liberty when free born men
Having to advise the public may speak free,
Which he who can, and will, deserv's high praise,
Who neither can nor will, may hold his peace;
What can be juster in a State then this?
Euripid. Hicetid.

Noutmb 24. LONDON,
Printed in the Yeare, 1644.

John Milton's Areopagitica *is considered one of the most eloquent pleas for freedom of the press ever written. Milton, a poet, wrote* Paradise Lost.

Seditious Libel

By contemporary standards, however, freedom of the press was still a long way off. Although the government no longer interfered with material before it was published (which is called **prior censorship**), it could still take stern measures after publication.

By the time government licensing ended in England, the common law courts had enacted the law of **seditious libel**. This law made it a crime to publish anything that might provoke hatred of or contempt for the king or the government. Furthermore, it was illegal to print anything that would stir up discontent among the king's subjects or cause them to challenge any rule of church or state in an illegal way. The wording of the law was so unclear that any criticism of the government or its policies, however well founded, could be considered a violation.

In seditious libel cases, publishers could be jailed even if what they printed about officials was true. In fact, true criticisms were considered greater crimes, since they were far more damaging to the government's reputation than false criticism. In other words, anyone who published a story claiming that an official was dishonest was guilty of seditious libel. The crime was even more serious if the official really was dishonest!

Seditious libel law was used not only to stifle criticism of government officials, but also to restrict reporters' ability to gather news. Simply reporting an official's actions could be declared seditious libel if the official did not want the action reported. Newspapers were not allowed to report on debates in Parliament until 1771.

The law of seditious libel was not seriously challenged in England during the early 18th century. Most people believed that unrestricted criticism of the government was harmful to the country, if not downright treasonous.

In the reconstructed colonial village in Williamsburg, Virginia, a printing and post office has been recreated. Shown here is the press room, located in the basement.

3
The Press in Colonial America

Printing in colonial America was even more strictly regulated than in England. Licensing of presses and censorship of printed material was enforced in the colonies for several decades after such practices had ended in England. The secret presses that had undermined licensing in England never got started in America. The only presses in colonial America were shipped over from England and strictly accounted for. Also, demand for news was not great in the colonies, where the new inhabitants were preoccupied with the problems of settling the land.

Harvard College imported the first press to the Americas in 1638. All of the colonial governments eventually furnished money for presses. These early presses produced almanacs, textbooks, legal forms, and government laws. The government sent out information using these presses, so nothing controversial or critical of the government was printed.

Fifty years after Harvard received its press, an attempt was made to start the first newspaper in America. Benjamin Harris, a former London bookseller and publisher, opened a combined coffeehouse and bookshop in Boston. From there Harris issued a four-page newspaper, called *Publick Occurrences, Both Forreign and Domestick*, in 1690. The paper was to be published once a month "or if any Glut of Occurrences happen, oftener."

That turned out to be wishful thinking. Massachusetts authorities were offended by several articles in the first issue, including gossip about the king of France and an account of the torture of French captives by Indian allies of the British during the French and Indian wars. Since Harris had not obtained a license for his newspaper, shutting down his press was simple. Four days after the first issue appeared, the Massachusetts governor and council ordered Harris to cease publication.

Boston postmaster John Campbell learned from Harris's mistakes. When Campbell started his *Boston News-Letter* in 1702, he submitted all of his articles to the authorities for approval before printing. This strategy enabled the *News-Letter*, America's first continuously published newspaper, to survive for 72 years.

Rough Times for a Free Press

Even after prior censorship (licensing) was discontinued in the American colonies in the early 18th century, the press had to be wary. Court cases involving seditious libel were rare, but the law was in full force. Local authorities could invoke the law of seditious libel against anyone

When he was 12 years old, Benjamin Franklin became an apprentice to his older brother James, a printer. The two men published the New-England Courant.

who criticized the government. Any printer who challenged the law faced the threat of fines, jail sentences, whipping, and even branding.

The few cases that made it to the courts offered little hope for those accused of seditious libel. In 1721 the *New-England Courant* tested the waters of tolerance. Published by James Franklin, the older brother of Benjamin, this paper occasionally poked fun at authorities. Many readers particularly enjoyed the

The first continuously published newspaper in the colonies was The Boston News-Letter, *started by John Campbell, a postmaster.*

remarks aimed at stern Puritan religious leaders such as Increase Mather and his son Cotton. The government, however, took offense against a news report published in August of 1721. Colonial leaders thought the article implied that they were responding weakly to a pirate raid.

The printer was called before the Royal Council in 1722 on a charge of contempt. He remained outspoken and was thrown into jail. Eventually Franklin was freed under the condition that he never again publish a newspaper or pamphlet. Although he defied that order by naming his brother Benjamin publisher, James decided to stop criticizing the authorities. The paper remained entertaining, but was not nearly as daring as it had been.

Zenger: The First Breakthrough

John Peter Zenger was an unlikely candidate to become a hero in the fight for a free press. The German immigrant was simply trying to make a living by running a printing press when he was caught in the crossfire of a political power struggle.

The trouble began when a group of New York citizens asked Zenger to edit a newspaper that would express their views. The group was opposed to the dictatorial leadership of the colony's British governor, Sir William Cosby. Zenger's print shop began printing the *New York Weekly Journal* in 1733. The newspaper contained scathing criticism of Governor Cosby.

Although the paper was written by others, it was printer Zenger who was held responsible for the contents. He was arrested under a charge of attempting to bring Governor Cosby and other officials into suspicion and the ill opinion of the people—seditious libel. Zenger was put in jail for several months.

At the trial, which began in 1735, Zenger seemed to have no chance. Following the legal tradition of the time, the jury was told that its only task was to determine whether or not Zenger had printed the material. The judge would decide if the words were libelous. Since Cosby had hand-picked the judge for the trial, the outcome seemed obvious.

To defend Zenger, his supporters called in Andrew Hamilton of Philadelphia, who was regarded as one of the best lawyers in America. Hamilton's clever strategy was to ignore the judges and speak directly to the jury. He surprised the court by admitting that Zenger *had* printed the newspaper. He then noted that,

Andrew Hamilton spoke out for freedom of the press at the trial of John Peter Zenger in 1735.

according to the official charges, the printer had been accused of publishing false material. If the newspaper articles about Cosby were not false, Hamilton argued, there could be no libel. Hamilton even offered to prove that the articles were true.

Outraged, the New York attorney general reminded the jury that under the law, the judgment about libel was none of their concern. They could only determine whether Zenger had published the paper—which he had already admitted. But Hamilton insisted that the jury could only find Zenger guilty if the stories in his paper were false. "The question before the court…." he argued, "is not the cause of the poor printer…. No! It is the best cause. It is the cause of liberty…. the liberty—both of exposing and opposing arbitrary power… by speaking and writing—truth."

The jury returned a verdict of not

Angry colonists burn stamped paper to protect the Stamp Act. Publishers had to pay a special tax to buy the paper.

served notice that public opinion had turned solidly against the idea of "the greater the truth, the greater the libel." The right to criticize public officials was gaining strength.

The Press and the Revolution

Even after the Zenger trial, most colonial newspapers kept a respectful distance from the affairs of the government. That all changed, however, after the British government began imposing taxes on the American colonies. The first attempt to levy a tax was the Stamp Act, passed in 1765. This required that all books, newspapers, official papers, and legal documents be written on officially stamped paper. In order to buy this paper, publishers had to pay a special tax.

The tax hit colonial newspaper publishers especially hard. Many were barely making a living and simply could not afford to pay the tax. Rather than violate the law, they shut down their presses. But other publishers reacted angrily. Two of the most outspoken newspapers were the *Boston Gazette* and the *Massachusetts Spy*. Samuel Adams, writing for the *Gazette*, made it clear that it wasn't just the extra financial burden that angered Americans. He declared

guilty, on the grounds that the articles Zenger printed were true and therefore not libel. Since a jury's decision cannot change the law, the Zenger case did not strike down the law of seditious libel. But it advanced freedom of the press in several ways. The case proved that the people could successfully protest abusive government actions. It increased the jury's power.

Most importantly, the Zenger case

When the British government tried a second time to levy a tax on colonial Americans in 1767, under the Townshend Acts, the press reacted swiftly. A journalist named John Dickinson began writing a series of articles for the *Pennsylvania Chronicle*. Dickinson argued that the British Parliament had no right to tax Americans without consulting them. "Let these truths be indelibly impressed on our minds:" Dickinson wrote, "that we cannot

John Dickinson earned the nickname "Penman of the Revolution" for his essays opposing British taxation.

that the actions of the British government posed a threat to the liberty that was the right of all free men.

The British government backed down in the face of the open revolt. But even though the Stamp Act was repealed within a year of its passage, some of the damage could not be undone. The American press had been aroused and had become the champion of freedom and American patriotism. Never again would it quietly sit by while the government went about its work.

Thomas Paine urged colonists to demand independence from England in his slim pamphlet Common Sense.

COMMON SENSE:
ADDRESSED TO THE
INHABITANTS
OF
AMERICA.
On the following interesting
SUBJECTS.

I. Of the Origin and Design of Government in general,
with concise Remarks on the English Constitution.

II. Of Monarchy and Hereditary Succession.

III. Thoughts on the present State of American Affairs.

IV. Of the present Ability of America, with some miscellaneous
Reflections.

Written by an ENGLISHMAN.

By Thomas Paine

Man knows no Master save creating HEAVEN,
Or those whom choice and common good ordain.
THOMSON.

PHILADELPHIA, Printed
And Sold by R. BELL, in Third-Street. 1776.

"The birthday of a new world is at hand," Paine wrote in **Common Sense.**

be happy without being free." Entitled "Letters from a Farmer in Pennsylvania to the Inhabitants of the British Colonies," the bold essays were reprinted in most of the colonial newspapers and were so widely read that Dickinson was known as the "Penman of the Revolution."

While colonial Americans stood solidly against the taxation efforts of the British government, they disagreed about what to do about the situation. Englishman Thomas Paine helped swing the balance toward revolution when he arrived in Philadelphia in 1774. After observing the struggle for freedom in England and America, Paine came to believe that Americans could only gain their rights by separating from England. Paine published his views in a pamphlet called *Common Sense,* published in January 1776. "Until an independence is declared," he said, "the continent will feel itself like a man who continues putting off some unpleasant business from day to day, yet knows it must be done...."

Within three months, 120,000 copies of *Common Sense* had been sold. In a country that contained fewer than four million people, the pamphlet must have had an enormous impact. By July of that year, so many Americans supported separation from England that the colonies declared their independence.

4
Free Press and the Constitution

The colonies finally won their long and often discouraging war for independence from England in 1783. By this time the importance of a free press was clear. When the founders of the new nation met to write its Constitution, there were few debates about freedom of the press. Having felt the sting of repression, the founders of the United States of America knew that freedom of information and freedom to criticize the government were necessary in a democracy. The First Amendment to the Constitution stated that Congress could make no law abridging freedom of speech or of the press.

Yet the treatment of Tories (those who remained loyal to the British government) during the Revolutionary War indicated that freedom of the press was not absolute. Although they had spoken out passionately for liberty before the war, during the war, many Americans only wanted freedom for those who supported the revolution. Newspapers that had remained loyal to England were shut down, and outspoken Tories faced imprisonment or tar and feathers. In addition, the law of seditious libel was still widely supported.

The Alien and Sedition Acts of 1798

Although the First Amendment guaranteed freedom of the press, it did not define what that freedom

At the Constitutional Convention, which met in Philadelphia in 1787, delegates drew up a new framework for the government. Two years later, James Madison added 10 amendments—the Bill of Rights—to the Constitution.

meant or establish the limits to that freedom. The absence of a clearly defined concept of freedom of the press caused turmoil. Seven years after the First Amendment prohibited Congress from passing any law abridging the freedom of the press, Congress passed just such a law.

The Alien and Sedition Acts of 1798 were passed because of a deep split between the leaders of the new United States government. The Federalists, led by Alexander Hamilton and John Adams, believed in a strong central or federal government. The Republicans, led by Thomas Jefferson and James

Madison, believed in a decentralized government that gave more power to individual states.

As the differences between the two parties grew more bitter, newspapers began to back one or the other party. Republican and Federalist newspapers exchanged heated attacks. As Federalist President Adams and Republican Vice-President Jefferson set their sights on the presidential election of 1800, what started out as a difference of opinion turned into a brutal war of words.

The Federalists were especially angered by remarks printed about President Adams. They did not believe that the First Amendment was meant to protect what they saw as a vicious, irresponsible press. A newspaper that printed articles damaging to someone's reputation had to be held accountable. The Federalists—who controlled the legislature—responded by passing the Alien and Sedition Acts of 1798.

The Sedition Act made it a crime to "write, print, utter, or publish... any false, scandalous, and malicious criticism... against the government of the United States, or either house of the Congress... or the said President." In one respect, this was a step forward for freedom of the press. It upheld the Zenger tradition by declaring that only false criticism could be punished. But who would decide what was "false criticism"? For many Federalists, false criticism meant any criticism that they did not like. They used the act to harass and punish their Republican opponents. A Republican who expressed even such a mild opinion as wishing "peace and retirement to the President" (who was running for reelection) ran the risk of arrest.

Many Americans who had accepted the idea of some government control of the press had second thoughts. The Federalists were, in effect, outlawing any newspaper that did not agree with them. What had happened to freedom of the press? Alarmed at the evidence of abuse by the ruling party, many people began to think about the issue more carefully.

Public opinion turned so strongly against the Federalists that Republican Thomas Jefferson was elected president in 1800, and the Federalists faded away as a political force. Jefferson pardoned all those who had been convicted under the Sedition Act. The act was allowed to expire in 1801.

Jefferson's Turn

Ironically, it was a Federalist, Alexander Hamilton, who took the United States on its next step toward a free press, and it was Thomas Jefferson who tried to curb that freedom. During his presidency, Jefferson began to receive some of the same kind of vicious criticism that had so enraged John Adams. Jefferson did not like it any better than Adams had.

Although Jefferson had argued that the federal government could not abridge the freedom of the press, he didn't try to stop state governments from doing that. Despite the ideas set forth in the Constitution,

Federalist leader Alexander Hamilton fought Jefferson on many issues, including freedom of the press. Hamilton was later killed in a duel with Aaron Burr, who had been vice-president under Jefferson.

many state laws still upheld the old notion that even truthful criticism of officials could be libelous. Using these state laws of seditious libel, Jefferson had a number of his critics arrested and brought to trial. In a New York case, *The People v. Croswell*, Federalist leader Alexander Hamilton proclaimed that truth published "with good motives, for justifiable ends" was a defense against accusations of libel.

Although Hamilton lost the case, his eloquent argument for a free press swayed the New York Legislature. In 1805 it passed a law incorporating Hamilton's rule of truth as a libel defense. Many states quickly followed New York's lead.

The controversy over the passage of the Sedition Act and Jefferson's actions led the United States people to think carefully about the meaning of a free press. The U.S. tradition of a free press was established early on and has held strong ever since.

5
Changes in the United States Press

Most United States newspaper editors in the 19th century enjoyed virtually unlimited freedom to print criticism of public officials, except during times of war. The government encouraged the spread of information to the public by offering cheap postal rates for newspapers. This made it possible for people with little money to publish small newspapers. The number of newspapers published in the United States mushroomed from about 200 in 1800 to 1,200 by 1830.

The wide variety of reading material available increased the public's interest in reading, which boosted newspaper circulation. Increased circulations, in turn, led to higher profits for newspapers from the sale of advertising space. The newspaper, once only a small part of a printer's business, became a business in itself. Newspaper publishers and editors searched for ways to increase their number of readers and their profits.

In 1833 a young New York printer named Benjamin Day began publishing the *New York Sun*. The paper was unusual because it sold for only a penny; it was the United States' first successful penny newspaper, and it started a new trend in journalism. The *Sun* reported everyday happenings in the city as well as the usual political news. It was also the first U.S. newspaper to cover police news regularly.

The popular success of the *Sun* prodded other papers to test fresh

ideas of what was newsworthy. James Gordon Bennett started the *New York Herald* in 1835. He outdid the *Sun* with even more colorful, lively, and inventive stories. Bennett's Wall Street and society features were the forerunners of modern financial and society pages.

Several years later, two other New York papers appeared that set new standards of quality for journalism.

Two important 19th-century newspapermen: Benjamin Henry Day (top) and James Gordon Bennett, Jr. (bottom)

A drawing shows the pressroom of the New York Tribune *in the 19th century.*

The *New York Tribune* was founded in 1841 by Horace Greeley. Although it was originally published as a voice for the Whig party, the *Tribune* put great effort into reporting news decently and fairly. Greeley's editorials—particularly his passionate pleas to end slavery—gained such respect and influence that he was later chosen by the Democratic party to run against Ulysses Grant in the 1872 presidential campaign. The *New York Times* provided similar high-quality news at an inexpensive price.

As the United States continued to expand, industrialization and the rise of the factory system turned small cities into busy metropolitan areas. Demand for daily city newspapers grew rapidly. During the late 19th century, many large newspapers were launched to meet this demand.

Eventually, the competition between newspapers became fierce. In an effort to maintain sales, many U.S. newspapers drifted away from standards of fairness and decency toward **sensationalism**, which provoked a quick, usually superficial emotion in the reader.

In 1883 Joseph Pulitzer, a successful publisher from St. Louis,

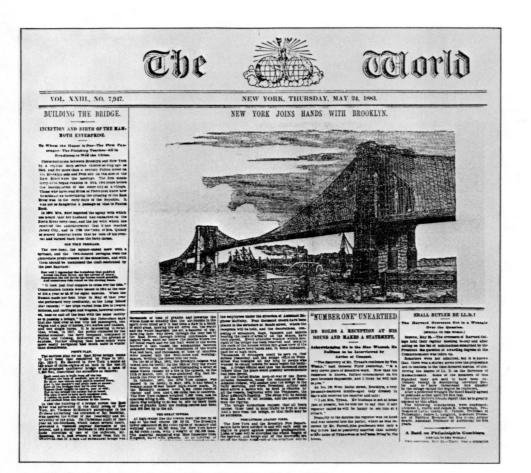

Joseph Pulitzer bought the New York World *in 1883.*

Missouri, purchased the *New York World*. A circulation war broke out between the *New York Journal*, which William Randolph Hearst took over in 1895, and Pulitzer's *New York World*. These papers spawned an irresponsible style of reporting that became known as "yellow journalism" because of the yellow ink used by the papers in their rival comic sections. Both the *Journal* and the *World* resorted to sensationalist tactics in an effort to attract readers. Large, screaming headlines called attention to stories of spectacular crime, scandal, divorce, and gossip. Sometimes stories were spiced up with false interviews and faked pictures.

Yellow journalism peaked just before the Spanish-American War in 1898. The *Journal* and the *World* found that stories of atrocities allegedly committed by Spanish forces in Cuba helped sell newspapers. William Randolph Hearst helped turn public opinion against Spain when he published a private letter written by the Spanish ambassador in Washington. The letter spoke of President William McKinley in unflattering terms.

When the United States battleship *Maine* exploded and sank in the harbor of Havana, Cuba, on February 15, 1898, the *Journal* and other U.S. papers blamed Spain for the incident. Although there was no evidence to back up the accusation, the *Journal* helped popularize the slogan "Remember the Maine." This became the rallying cry of those who, like Hearst, wanted to see the United States at war with Spain. As Hearst had hoped, war did come, and the reports from war correspondents helped sell newspapers.

Even some of the more scrupulous

Joseph Pulitzer (left) and William Randolph Hearst did battle through their newspapers.

$50,000 REWARD.—WHO DESTROYED THE MAINE?—$50,000 REWARD.

EDITION FOR GREATER NEW YORK

NEW YORK JOURNAL
AND ADVERTISER.

NO. 5,572.   NEW YORK, THURSDAY, FEBRUARY 17, 1898.—16 PAGES.   PRICE ONE CENT

DESTRUCTION OF THE WAR SHIP MAINE WAS THE WORK OF AN ENEMY.

$50,000!
$50,000 REWARD!
For the Detection of the
Perpetrator of
the Maine Outrage!

Assistant Secretary Roosevelt Convinced the Explosion of the War Ship Was Not an Accident.

The Journal Offers $50,000 Reward for the Conviction of the Criminals Who Sent 258 American Sailors to Their Death. Naval Officers Unanimous That the Ship Was Destroyed on Purpose.

$50,000!
$50,000 REWARD!
For the Detection of the
Perpetrator of
the Maine Outrage!

NAVAL OFFICERS THINK THE MAINE WAS DESTROYED BY A SPANISH MINE.

Hidden Mine or a Sunken Torpedo Believed to Have Been the Weapon Used Against the American Man-of-War---Officers and Men Tell Thrilling Stories of Being Blown Into the Air Amid a Mass of Shattered Steel and Exploding Shells---Survivors Brought to Key West Scout the Idea of Accident---Spanish Officials Protest Too Much---Our Cabinet Orders a Searching Inquiry---Journal Sends Divers to Havana to Report Upon the Condition of the Wreck.
Was the Vessel Anchored Over a Mine?

BY CAPTAIN E. L. ZALINSKI, U.S.A.

Assistant Secretary of the Navy Theodore Roosevelt says he is convinced that the destruction of the Maine in Havana Harbor was not an accident. The Journal offers a reward of $50,000 for exclusive evidence that will convict the person, persons or Government criminally responsible for the destruction of the American battle ship and the death of 258 of its crew.

The suspicion that the Maine was deliberately blown up grows stronger every hour. Not a single fact to the contrary has been produced.

Captain Sigsbee, of the Maine, and Consul-General Lee both urge that public opinion be suspended until they have completed their investigation. They are taking the course of tactful men who are convinced that there has been treachery.

Washington reports very late that Captain Sigsbee had feared some such event as a hidden mine. The English cipher code was used all day yesterday by the naval officers in cabling instead of the usual American code.

The sensationalism of Hearst's **New York Journal** *peaked after the sinking of the battleship* **Maine.**

newspapers borrowed certain yellow journalism techniques, such as huge headlines. Other publishers held to higher standards. Adolph Ochs, who took over the *New York Times* in 1896, was one such person. In 1898 he challenged the yellow journals by cutting the price of the *Times* from three cents to a penny. With the lower price and solid news coverage, the *Times* attracted many more readers and advertisers. In one year, circulation tripled, to 75,000 readers in 1899. Ochs proved that a newspaper could avoid sensationalism and still make a large profit.

Early in the 20th century, many newspaper editors recognized that they had broad powers to influence public opinion. They believed that freedom and responsibility must go hand in hand. Editors and publishers formed associations in which codes of ethics were developed. Most newspapers gradually stopped using yellow journalism techniques.

One kind of newspaper, however, continued to rely on sensationalism to sell papers. These newspapers, called **tabloids**, were printed on smaller-sized pages than other newspapers, with much of the space reserved for photographs. Early tabloids, which first appeared in 1919, were generally regarded as "scandal

Adolph Ochs set high standards for the **New York Times.**

sheets." Tabloids have not changed much since then.

Widespread changes in the press occurred in the early to mid-20th century with the invention of new forms of mass communication. The "press" has been expanded to include far more than printed materials such as newspapers, books, and magazines. Radio, television, and motion pictures are all ways of presenting ideas or information to mass audiences. Because of the growing influence of the media, United States citizens are continually reexamining the laws regarding freedom of the press. While court cases concerning freedom of the press were relatively rare before the 20th century, they have been important throughout this century.

Many people believe that some limits must be placed on freedom of the press during times of war.

6
Freedom of the Press Issues

The questions that arise concerning freedom of the press are rarely easy to answer. In the 20th century, many issues of freedom of the press have been debated in the Supreme Court. The Supreme Court determines the meaning of the Constitution and whether or not laws passed by Congress are allowed by the Constitution.

Legal scholars disagree about how the Constitution should be interpreted. Some people believe Constitutional law should be based on the original intent of the writers of the document. For others, the Constitution is a "living document" and must change as society changes. For example, the Constitution originally did not grant voting rights to black people or women.

Before 1925 the Supreme Court refused to get involved with matters of state law. But in 1925 the Court ruled that the 14th Amendment to the Constitution protected freedom of speech and the press against violation by state as well as federal laws.

Over the years, the Court has offered various interpretations of the freedom of the press clause of the First Amendment. The opinions of the Court justices have changed, but they have helped focus the debate by providing clear, thoughtful reasons for limiting or refusing to limit speech in particular cases. What follows are descriptions of some important issues concerning freedom of the press.

1. CENSORSHIP

Mob Censorship

On rare occasions, individual citizens have disregarded the law and appointed themselves as public censors of the press. The worst example of this took place in the 1830s. Several times, pro-slavery mobs destroyed or dismantled the presses of those who printed anti-slavery newspapers. In 1837 in Alton, Illinois, Elijah Lovejoy, publisher of an abolitionary newspaper, was murdered while defending his press against a mob attack.

The Post Office as Censor

One of the thorniest First Amendment problems for legal scholars has

Mobs attack a press that printed antislavery material. Censorship by pro-slavery mobs happened several times during the 1830s.

been the role of the Post Office in censoring materials that are sent through the mail. Does the Bill of Rights protect the right to send anything through the mail? Or can the postal service refuse to distribute materials the government considers harmful?

In 1835 President Andrew Jackson asked Congress to pass a law that would prohibit the mailing of antislavery publications to Southern states. Southern slave owners feared antislavery groups' mailing out literature calling on slaves to revolt.

Senator John C. Calhoun of South Carolina followed up on Jackson's request. He proposed legislation that would give the Post Office the power to refuse to circulate newspapers or other literature that advocated the abolition of slavery. Senator Daniel Webster of Massachusetts opposed the bill, saying it violated the First Amendment. A majority of Congress sided with Webster, and the Calhoun bill was defeated. Postmasters in Southern states, however, simply refused to deliver antislavery newspapers.

During the Civil War, the postmaster general began removing anti-Union material from the mail. Congress added to the postmaster general's powers by outlawing ob-

Montgomery Blair was postmaster general in 1835.

scene material from the mail in 1865 and lottery materials in 1868. Over the next half century, the Supreme Court upheld the laws giving censorship powers to the postal system. An 1892 decision held that the postal ban on obscene materials was not censorship, since it did not prevent a publisher from printing the materials.

When the United States entered World War I, many people believed that it was every citizen's patriotic duty to support the war effort. The

41

During World War I, newspapers written in a foreign language had to provide translations to the Post Office. Shown at left is a Yiddish daily paper, **Forward.** **The Masses** *(right) could not be mailed out during the war.*

Post Office became a prime weapon in the fight to restrict freedom of the press to "acceptable" opinions. The Espionage Act of 1917 barred from the mails any publication that might cause disloyalty or obstruct the recruitment of soldiers. The Trading-with-the-Enemy Act, passed by Congress the same year, allowed local postmasters to demand certified translations of newspaper or magazine articles written in a foreign language. Since the United States was at war with Germany, this act was primarily aimed at German-language newspapers, some of which were sympathetic to Germany.

In 1918 Congress passed the Sedition Act. This law made it a crime to write or publish any disloyal, profane, or abusive language about the government of the United States. Publishing articles favorable to any country at war with the United States was also forbidden.

The Post Office Department used

these three acts to exercise vast powers. Some newspapers, such as the socialist *New York Call* and the *Milwaukee Leader*, were refused mailing privileges, as was the socialist magazine *The Masses*. Other publications were allowed to use the mails only by agreeing to print nothing about the war. About half of the German-language newspapers stopped publishing. The Sedition Act was repealed in 1921, but not before hundreds of people had been jailed for expressing their opinions.

Over the years, the Post Office was gradually stripped of some of its powers. In 1946 the Supreme Court was asked to rule whether the Post Office Department had the right to withdraw *Esquire* magazine's second-class mailing privilege. A Post Office official had claimed that the lower cost of second-class mail could be used only by those who made a "special contribution to the public welfare." In the official's opinion, *Esquire* did not merit that description.

Faced with postal bills a half-million dollars higher than other magazines paid, *Esquire* appealed to the Supreme Court. The Court ruled that "to withdraw the second-class rate from this publication today because its contents seem to one official not good for the public would sanction withdrawals of the second-class rate tomorrow from another periodical whose social or economic views seemed harmful to another official." The decision limited the Post Office's role as a censor. The Post Office can still refuse to deliver a particular issue of a publication, but it cannot make decisions about material that has not yet been printed.

The Government as Censor

Throughout the 19th century, the government rarely interfered directly with the efforts of publishers—except during times of war. Some presses were shut down during the Civil War. There was also some censorship of outgoing telegraph and cable correspondence during the Spanish-American War.

The restriction of freedoms during World War I reflected a widespread belief that some form of government control over the press, including censorship, was necessary at times. This belief clashed with the idea that any law giving the government control over information was expressly prohibited by the First Amendment.

The cases that generated the most heated debate concerned periodicals that abused the freedom of the

The Saturday Press

Vol. 1, No. 9　　　　Minneapolis, Minn., Nov. 19, 1927　　　　Price 5 Cents

A "Close-Up" View Of the City Hall

"Big Mose" Tries to "Smart-up" the Chief, But Found No Brains; Chief Claims He Saved Mayor From Jail and Mayor's Buddy Tries to Find a New Chief. How the Lice Swarmed as in the Days of Egypt, Until They Over-ran the Fixer's Patience. And Some Fodder for Floyd's Mental Silo.

Dawn—and the deep purple of the firmament melted, and gave way to the irresistible rays of Old Sol. The sombre colors of night faded out to make room for the colors of a new day—the gold and silver and green (long green) of a loyalty administration. But soon the fiery bolts of Jupiter were shot across a sky which was no longer clear, political meteors crashed and chaos ruled in Polk's Center, for a greasy Jew had soaped the tracks and a hand car was running wild.

Brunskill, to show his undying appreciation to Mose for keeping bank robbers from robbing banks in Minneapolis, had cut Mose in on protected gambling. And Mose, to show his undying appreciation to Brunskill for cutting him in on gambling, put the bank robbers to work hauling alcohol by truck loads and 'tis hinted about head quarters that he cut the chief in on that.

Be that as it may, the light ning hit for McCormick is and was a mighty good business man His office was appointive and not elective. His duty it was to fetch to the City Hall

Demoralizing Our Police Force

Mayor Leach Suspends Patrolman for Tagging Mayor's Car, Then Reinstates and "Delivers Lecture on Courtesy." Is Leach Immune From the Law Bill Jones Is Forced to Obey? Can a Hans Schmit Be Fined and a Leach Feted for Violation of the Same Law? If so, Why?

In other issues, I have called attention to the demoralization of the rank and file of our police department. I have charged that the MEN dare not obey an order lest in obeying they offend one of their superior officers or a "sacred cow" of the administration and find themselves minus a job or in serious trouble. The favorite pastime of the brainless wonders at the head of our present administration police and ex routine of discipline and de

rial stadium during a football game was instructed to tag every car left in a nonparking zone. He wasn't given orders to tag this car and slip that bus. He was told to tag ALL cars left in nonparking zones and being a good officer, he obeyed orders

Our mayor is a football enthusiast and he "took in" the game. He also left his car in a nonparking zone

"His" subordinate, under orders from his superior tagged the mayor's car. And what

To many people, the Saturday Press *was just another "scandal sheet." But the paper's publisher, Jay Near, won his case in the Supreme Court and established an important principle for freedom of the press.*

44

press by printing lies and articles that damaged people's reputations. During the 1920s, such journalistic abuse had multiplied. Many of the "scandal sheet" tabloids littered the newsstands with outrageous, irresponsible stories. In Minnesota, public disgust with these papers led to the passing of the "Minnesota gag law" in 1925. This law gave judges the power to stop publication of obscene, scandalous, or **defamatory** (harmful to someone's reputation) articles.

In 1927 the gag law was invoked against the *Saturday Press*, a small Minneapolis paper that used racial slurs, called the police "rodents," and hurled incredible accusations at police and other local officials. Minneapolis officials obtained a restraining order stopping publication of the *Saturday Press*.

The publishers of the paper brought the case to court. Finally the case, *Near v. Minnesota*, reached the Supreme Court. In a split decision, the Court ruled in favor of the *Saturday Press*. It declared, "The fact that the liberty of the press may be abused by miscreant purveyors of scandal does not make any the less necessary the immunity of the press from previous restraint...." In the eyes of the law, the public's right to obtain information without government interference was so important that it had to be guaranteed to everyone, even those who used that freedom irresponsibly.

The Pentagon Papers

The Pentagon Papers case brought up the question of whether the government can prevent publication of material to protect national security.

In 1971 the *New York Times* obtained secret government documents. The documents were part of a study that had been ordered by former Secretary of Defense Robert McNamara concerning the Vietnam War. All the information in the papers, which became known as the Pentagon Papers, concerned past administrations. The *New York Times* decided that none of the secrets in the papers would harm the current war effort. On June 13, 1971, it published the first installment of a series of articles that quoted the Pentagon Papers.

Attorney General John Mitchell asked the *Times* to stop publishing the papers. When the *Times* continued publishing the series, the government took the paper to court. Citing national security concerns, a

Cartoonist Patrick Oliphant celebrated the defeat of Attorney General John Mitchell in the Pentagon Papers case.

judge issued an order temporarily restraining the newspaper from publishing the Pentagon Papers until the case could be studied further.

Three days later, excerpts from the Pentagon Papers appeared in the *Washington Post*. This paper, too, was taken to court. Because of the urgency of the case, it was taken up by the Supreme Court almost immediately.

Over the years, the Supreme Court had attempted to clearly define freedom of the press. In the *Near* case, the Court had found no excuse for government censorship. Yet at other times, the Court had recognized situations in which freedom of the press could be restricted.

On June 30, 1971, the Court ruled 6-3 that the government's attempt to stop the *Times* and the *Post* from publishing the Pentagon Papers was a violation of the First Amendment. Many of the justices made it clear that their decision did not mean that the government could never interfere with the press. The majority decided, however, that the Pentagon Papers did not pose enough of a threat to the government to justify the invasion of the rights of the press.

Most magazines that are considered pornographic are not sold to minors.

More recently, the Court has upheld selected cases of government censorship. In 1979 an article describing how easy it was to make a hydrogen bomb appeared in *The Progressive* magazine. The government was able to stop publication of the article for a short time. In 1980 the Supreme Court ruled against former CIA (Central Intelligence Agency) agent Frank Snepp, who had written a book detailing the final days before the Communist takeover of South Vietnam. The government said that Snepp had violated a CIA rule that any material published by former employees had to be cleared first with the CIA. Snepp's lawyers argued that this was government censorship and violated the First Amendment.

The Supreme Court upheld a judgment against Snepp. According to the Court, the need for secrecy in intelligence operations was so important that it took priority over the First Amendment.

Where pornography and obscenity are concerned, many U.S. citizens believe that the public welfare is more important than the First Amendment. In obscenity cases, however, the courts have been wary of allowing the government to assume powers of censorship. There have been some exceptions to this rule, especially regarding the sale of pornographic material to minors. Throughout the 1980s, legislatures and city officials have continued to search for ways to limit the influence of pornography without infringing on the freedom of the press.

II. THE RIGHT TO PRINT CRITICISM

Contempt of Court

Contempt of court means showing disrespect for the authority or dignity of a court of law. Contempt of court has long been considered a valid exception to the right of free speech. It is punishable by law.

In the early days of the nation, a judge could declare a publisher in contempt for printing a news article that offended the judge. Congress put a stop to this in 1831. It passed a law that restricted contempt of court judgments to cases in which the "offender" was actually present in court or causing an obstruction of justice. In 1941 the Supreme Court affirmed that a newspaper could not be held in contempt unless its comments on court proceedings created a clear and present danger to the administration of justice.

Sedition

During a war, citizens' fears about the safety of their country increase. Often people distrust anyone who criticizes the government.

During World War I, many people in the United States feared that speaking or writing negatively about the war would cause the U.S. to lose. Many people wrote letters to Congress asking for stronger laws. That was one reason why Congress passed the 1918 Sedition Act. The wording of this law was so vague that it was used to outlaw any criticism of the government.

The government's right to protect itself from danger was upheld by the Supreme Court in 1919. In the case of *Schenck v. the United States*, the Court ruled that Congress could restrict the freedom of the press if it was determined that a publication posed a "clear and present danger" to the government.

In his landmark opinion, Justice Oliver Wendell Holmes spelled out the "clear and present danger" test. He said that it is impossible to judge whether statements are legal or illegal without taking into account the circumstances surrounding the statement. A statement that would be harmless in peacetime might cause problems when the country is at war. The crucial test, according to Holmes, was whether the words

In the 1930s, Louisiana governor Huey P. Long tried to tax the state's newspapers as a punishment to his opponents.

caused an immediate, obvious danger to the country's well-being.

At first the Supreme Court upheld most convictions of persons prosecuted under the Sedition Act. Eventually, following the leadership of Justice Holmes, the courts and legislatures shifted their stances to allow greater freedom to criticize the government. In 1921 the Sedition Act was repealed. Four years later, the Supreme Court ruled that state governments must guarantee freedom of the press as fully as the federal government does.

In the 1930s, Louisiana Governor Huey Long's attempt to muzzle his critics was struck down by the Supreme Court. Long had placed a special tax on the advertising income of larger Louisiana daily newspapers —papers that opposed Long's administration. In the case of *Grosjean v. American Press*, the Court decided that Long's methods amounted to a tax on knowledge, which had been ruled out since the time of the American Revolution.

A newspaper copy desk in the 1940s. By then, the press could criticize the government without fear of censorship or punishment.

By the 1940s, the press was free to criticize the government in all but the most blatant instances of incitement to criminal acts. During World War II, the media enjoyed far greater freedom to criticize than they had in World War I, without harm to the country's ability to wage war.

Shortly after World War II, however, many United States people saw a new threat to their security. The Communist movement that had swept the Soviet Union in 1917 was spreading to other countries. Many people feared that Communists would try to take over the United States and destroy the "American way of life."

The Smith Act of 1940, the first peacetime sedition act since 1798, made it illegal to advocate or teach the violent overthrow of any government in the United States. The act also made it illegal to print, publish, or distribute written material advocating the violent overthrow of any government in the United States. It outlawed the very type of publication that Thomas Paine had written to gather support for the founding of the country.

In the 1950s, fear of Communism

began to override concerns for free speech. In 1951 the Supreme Court, in a split decision, upheld the Smith Act, which had been cited against 11 leaders of the American Communist Party. In the case of *Dennis v. United States*, Chief Justice Fred Vinson wrote, "Overthrow of the Government by force and violence is certainly a substantial enough interest for the Government to limit speech." To Justice Vinson, a conspiracy to overthrow the government did present a "clear and present danger," and the freedom of speech and press of the Communist organization could be limited.

From 1950 to 1954, Joseph McCarthy, a senator from Wisconsin, fanned the fears of Communism. Week after week, McCarthy claimed he had fresh proof that Communists had infiltrated the government on all levels, right up to the State Department.

Such reports ignited suspicions about who was a Communist and who was not. People in the army, schoolteachers, labor union members, and even church officials were denounced as Communists. People were afraid to speak out for fear that they would also be accused of being Communists. Newspapers and magazines that dared to criticize

McCarthy lost subscribers and were subjected to harassment.

But McCarthy and his followers were not able to pass legislation restricting the longstanding right of the press to criticize public officials. In 1957 the Supreme Court said that it is not illegal to speak or write in favor of violent revolution. The changing opinions of the Supreme Court throughout the years show that the delicate balance between a free press and a secure country can be altered by public opinion.

Wisconsin Senator Joseph McCarthy (right) harassed newspapers that dared to oppose him. He accused his enemies of being Communists.

51

III. LIBEL

When published criticism of a person crosses the bounds of what is considered acceptable comment, it is subject to the laws of libel. Since libel laws differ from state to state, libel can be discussed only in general terms. **Libel** is a false and defamatory attack in written form on a person's character. (Broadcasting can also be considered libelous, since the material is written first. Speech that is false and defamatory is called **slander**.)

Libel of Public Officials

The First Amendment provides a great deal of protection to the press in cases involving libel of public officials or candidates for public office. This protection is considered necessary to ensure that the government will not restrict the flow of accurate information.

The first breakthrough in libel law was the 1805 New York law that declared that criticism of a public official cannot be considered libel if it is true and is published with good intentions. In 1837 the New Hampshire Supreme Court ruled that there can be no libel of public officials even if the material is published with the intention of hurting the official's reputation, provided the material is true.

State libel laws, however, varied considerably in the 19th century. Statements of opinion were one tricky area. In a libel case, it was up to the person who wrote the offending statements to prove that they were true. Since opinions could not be proved either false or true, government officials had the advantage.

The most important Supreme Court decision concerning libel of public officials did not take place until 1964. This case was *New York Times Co. v. Sullivan*. The dispute started with an advertisement entitled "Heed Their Rising Voices" placed in the March 29, 1960, edition of the *Times*. The ad was an appeal for money for the civil rights movement, in response to the arrest of Martin Luther King, Jr., in Montgomery, Alabama. The advertisement briefly described some of the events that had occurred in Montgomery. The main points of the description were accurate, but there were also several errors of fact.

Although he was not mentioned

After civil rights leader Martin Luther King, Jr., was arrested, a group of his supporters placed an advertisement appealing for money for the civil rights cause. The ad led to the case of **New York Times Co. v. Sullivan.**

by name in the advertisement, Montgomery Commissioner L.B. Sullivan considered the article an attack on him. Sullivan sued four individuals who had signed the advertisement, and the *New York Times.* At the trial, Sullivan's lawyer argued that advertisements are not protected by the First Amendment. The jury deliberated only two hours before finding in favor of Sullivan. Libel damages of $500,000 were awarded. That award was upheld by the Alabama Supreme Court.

The Supreme Court of the United States reversed the decision of the lower courts, however. The Court declared that, although commercial advertisements might not be fully protected by the First Amendment, "editorial advertisements" were. In the opinion of the Court, a decision in favor of Sullivan would discourage newspapers from carrying editorial advertisements "and so might shut off an important outlet for the promulgation [spread] of information and ideas by persons who do not themselves have access to publishing facilities...."

The Court dealt with the factual errors cited in the advertisement by

> *The growing movement of peaceful mass demonstrations by Negroes is something new in the South, something understandable....*
> *Let Congress heed their rising voices, for they will be heard.*
>
> —*New York Times* editorial
> Saturday, March 19, 1960

Heed Their Rising Voices

As the whole world knows by now, thousands of Southern Negro students are engaged in widespread non-violent demonstrations in positive affirmation of the right to live in human dignity as guaranteed by the U. S. Constitution and the Bill of Rights. In their efforts to uphold these guarantees, they are being met by an unprecedented wave of terror by those who would deny and negate that document which the whole world looks upon as setting the pattern for modern freedom....

In Orangeburg, South Carolina, when 400 students peacefully sought to buy doughnuts and coffee at lunch counters in the business district, they were forcibly ejected, tear-gassed, soaked to the skin in freezing weather with fire hoses, arrested en masse and herded into an open barbed-wire stockade to stand for hours in the bitter cold.

In Montgomery, Alabama, after students sang "My Country, 'Tis of Thee" on the State Capitol steps, their leaders were expelled from school, and truckloads of police armed with shotguns and tear-gas ringed the Alabama State College Campus. When the entire student body protested to state authorities by refusing to re-register, their dining hall was padlocked in an attempt to starve them into submission.

In Tallahassee, Atlanta, Nashville, Savannah, Greensboro, Memphis, Richmond, Charlotte, and a host of other cities in the South, young American teenagers, in face of the entire weight of official state apparatus and police power, have boldly stepped forth as protagonists of democracy. Their courage and amazing restraint have inspired millions and given a new dignity to the cause of freedom.

Small wonder that the Southern violators of the Constitution fear this new, non-violent brand of freedom fighter . . . even as they fear the upswelling right-to-vote movement. Small wonder that they are determined to destroy the one man who, more than any other, symbolizes the new spirit now sweeping the South—the Rev. Dr. Martin Luther King, Jr., world-famous leader of the Montgomery Bus Protest. For it is his doctrine of non-violence which has inspired and guided the students in their widening wave of sit-ins; and it is this same Dr. King who founded and is president of the Southern Christian Leadership Conference—the organization which is spearheading the surging right-to-vote movement. Under Dr. King's direction the Leadership Conference conducts Student Workshops and Seminars in the philosophy and technique of non-violent resistance.

Again and again the Southern violators have answered Dr. King's peaceful protests with intimidation and violence. They have bombed his home almost killing his wife and child. They have assaulted his person. They have arrested him seven times—for "speeding," "loitering" and similar "offenses." And now they have charged him with "perjury"—a *felony* under which they could imprison him for *ten years*. Obviously, their real purpose is to remove him physically as the leader to whom the students and millions of others—look for guidance and support, and thereby to intimidate *all* leaders who may rise in the South. Their strategy is to behead this affirmative movement, and thus to demoralize Negro Americans and weaken their will to struggle. The defense of Martin Luther King, spiritual leader of the student sit-in movement, clearly, therefore, is an integral part of the total struggle for freedom in the South.

Decent-minded Americans cannot help but applaud the creative daring of the students and the quiet heroism of Dr. King. But this is one of those moments in the stormy history of Freedom when men and women of good will must do more than applaud the rising-to-glory of others. The America whose good name hangs in the balance before a watchful world, the America whose heritage of Liberty these Southern Upholders of the Constitution are defending, is *our* America as well as theirs . . .

We must heed their rising voices—yes—but we must add our own.

We must extend ourselves above and beyond moral support and render the material help so urgently needed by those who are taking the risks, facing jail, and even death in a glorious re-affirmation of our Constitution and its Bill of Rights.

We urge you to join hands with our fellow Americans in the South by supporting, with your dollars, this Combined Appeal for all three needs—the defense of Martin Luther King—the support of the embattled students—and the struggle for the right-to-vote.

Your Help Is Urgently Needed . . . NOW !!

Stella Adler	Dr. Alan Knight Chalmers	Anthony Franciosa	John Killens	L. Joseph Overton	Maureen Stapleton
Raymond Pace Alexander	Richard Coe	Lorraine Hansbury	Eartha Kitt	Clarence Pickett	Frank Silvera
Harry Van Arsdale	Nat King Cole	Rev. Donald Harrington	Rabbi Edward Klein	Shad Polier	Hope Stevens
Harry Belafonte	Cheryl Crawford	Nat Hentoff	Hope Lange	Sidney Poitier	George Tabori
Julie Belafonte	Dorothy Dandridge	James Hicks	John Lewis	A. Philip Randolph	Rev. Gardner C.
Dr. Algernon Black	Ossie Davis	Mary Hinton	Viveca Lindfors	John Raitt	Taylor
Marc Blitzstein	Sammy Davis, Jr.	Van Heflin	Carl Murphy	Elmer Rice	Norman Thomas
William Branch	Ruby Dee	Langston Hughes	Don Murray	Jackie Robinson	Kenneth Tynan
Marlon Brando	Dr. Philip Elliott	Morris Iushewitz	John Murray	Mrs. Eleanor Roosevelt	Charles White
Mrs. Ralph Bunche	Dr. Harry Emerson	Mahalia Jackson	A. J. Muste	Bayard Rustin	Shelley Winters
Diahann Carroll	Fosdick	Mordecai Johnson	Frederick O'Neal	Robert Ryan	Max Youngstein

We in the south who are struggling daily for dignity and freedom warmly endorse this appeal

Rev. Ralph D. Abernathy (Montgomery, Ala.)	Rev. Matthew D. McCollom (Orangeburg, S. C.)	Rev. Walter L. Hamilton (Norfolk, Va.)	Rev. A. L. Davis (New Orleans, La.)
Rev. Fred L. Shuttlesworth (Birmingham, Ala.)	Rev. William Holmes Borders (Atlanta, Ga.)	I. S. Levy (Columbia, S. C.)	Mrs. Katie E. Whickham (New Orleans, La.)
Rev. Kelley Miller Smith (Nashville, Tenn.)	Rev. Douglas Moore (Durham, N. C.)	Rev. Martin Luther King, Sr. (Atlanta, Ga.)	Rev. W. H. Hall (Hattiesburg, Miss.)
Rev. W. A. Dennis (Chattanooga, Tenn.)	Rev. Wyatt Tee Walker (Petersburg, Va.)	Rev. Henry C. Bunton (Memphis, Tenn.) Rev. S. S. Seay, Sr. (Montgomery, Ala.)	Rev. J. E. Lowery (Mobile, Ala.)
Rev. C. K. Steele (Tallahassee, Fla.)		Rev. Samuel W. Williams (Atlanta, Ga.)	Rev. T. J. Jemison (Baton Rouge, La.)

COMMITTEE TO DEFEND MARTIN LUTHER KING AND THE STRUGGLE FOR FREEDOM IN THE SOUTH
312 West 125th Street, New York 27, N. Y. UNiversity 6-1700

Chairmen: A. Philip Randolph, Dr. Gardner C. Taylor; *Chairmen of Cultural Division:* Harry Belafonte, Sidney Poitier; *Treasurer:* Nat King Cole; *Executive Director:* Bayard Rustin; *Chairmen of Church Division:* Father George B. Ford, Rev. Harry Emerson Fosdick, Rev. Thomas Kilgore, Jr., Rabbi Edward E. Klein; *Chairman of Labor Division:* Morris Iushewitz.

Please mail this coupon TODAY!

> Committee To Defend Martin Luther King
> and
> The Struggle For Freedom In The South
> 312 West 125th Street, New York 27, N. Y.
> UNiversity 6-1700
>
> I am enclosing my contribution of $_____ for the work of the Committee.
>
> Name _____
> (PLEASE PRINT)
> Address _____
> City _____ Zone _____ State _____
>
> ☐ I want to help   ☐ Please send further information
>
> Please make checks payable to:
> Committee To Defend Martin Luther King

The Court said that "editorial advertisements" deserved First Amendment protection.

ruling that a public official cannot be paid damages for "a defamatory falsehood relating to his official conduct unless he proves that the statement was made with 'actual malice'—that is, with knowledge that it was false or with reckless disregard for whether it was false or not."

With these words, the Court added a new criterion to its test of whether a criticism of government officials was punishable. Not only did the words have to be false and cause damage to a person's reputation, they also had to be made with the knowledge that they were false, or with indifference as to whether or not they were false, and with the intention of causing harm.

These restrictions were necessary, the Court said, because "debate on public issues should be uninhibited, robust and wide-open...it may well include vehement, caustic and sometimes unpleasantly sharp attacks on government and public officials."

The *Sullivan* decision was hailed as a victory for a free press. For a time, a number of judges dismissed libel cases without even sending them to juries because of the difficulty of proving actual malice. Many people complained that this new interpretation of the law gave too much power to the press. But even

though the *Sullivan* decision reduced the number of libel lawsuits, it did not settle the issue.

The 1984-85 case brought by General William Westmoreland against CBS News offers some insights into the current state of libel law. In 1982 CBS News broadcast a television documentary called *The Uncounted Enemy: A Vietnam Deception.* The program accused United States military commanders in Vietnam of deliberately understating estimates of enemy troop strength. CBS concluded that the commanders had conspired to mislead U.S. civilian authorities into thinking that the United States and its allies were winning the war.

General William Westmoreland, who had been commander of United States forces in Vietnam from 1964 to 1968, denounced the broadcast as a lie. Upon reviewing the evidence, CBS admitted that "conspiracy" was too strong a word and that some of the normal newsgathering procedures had not been followed. But the network insisted that the basis of the broadcast was accurate. Westmoreland countered by filing a libel suit to clear his name.

After more than two years of preparation, however, Westmoreland withdrew his case. In return, CBS

General William Westmoreland dropped his libel case, but not before CBS had already spent a large sum of money to prepare its case.

issued a statement expressing its respect for Westmoreland's service and stressing that the producers of the documentary did not mean to imply that he had been disloyal or unpatriotic.

The amount of money CBS had to spend preparing a defense, however, caused anxiety among advocates of freedom of the press. A giant company such as CBS could afford to spend five million dollars to prepare a defense in a libel suit. But small

newspapers and book publishers would go broke trying to defend themselves in similar circumstances. Many journalists worry that the threat of libel has somewhat restricted a free press.

Libel and Private Individuals

The broad freedom to criticize public officials in the United States does not apply to private individuals. All 50 states and the District of Columbia have libel laws that protect the average citizen if reckless, false, or malicious information is published or broadcast about them. It is not necessary to prove actual malice in a libel case involving a private individual.

Libel and "Public Figures"

While libel laws clearly spell out the difference between libel of individuals and libel of public officials, they are less precise concerning an in-between category: public figures. A public figure is someone whose job or civic activity keeps him or her in the public eye. These people are not necessarily involved in government. Should they fall under the greater libel protections allowed individuals or under the narrower protections given to public officials?

In 1967 the Supreme Court debated this distinction in two similar cases. One case involved former University of Georgia Athletic Director Wally Butts. In 1963 an article in the *Saturday Evening Post* magazine claimed that Butts had passed some of his university's football secrets to Alabama coach Paul "Bear" Bryant. According to the *Post* story, Butts's secrets helped Alabama defeat Georgia in an important game. Butts sued the *Post* for libel, won his case, and was awarded $60,000.

In a 1967 decision, the Supreme Court upheld the judgment in favor of Butts. The Court found that the *Saturday Evening Post* had had plenty of time to find out if its story was true, yet had not made the slightest effort to do so. The Court concluded that such disregard satisfied the recently defined "actual malice" requirement. The question of whether or not Butts was a private citizen or a public official made no difference. The *Post* was guilty of libel even under the stringent rules applied to libel of public officials.

Another case brought before the Supreme Court that same year ended differently. Former Army Major General Edwin Walker had filed suit against the Associated Press

Wally Butts, who was athletic director at the University of Georgia, was falsely accused of fixing a football game.

(AP), a news service that sells stories to many newspapers throughout the country. A 1962 AP story had reported that Walker was involved in riots at the University of Mississippi. According to the report, Walker had led a crowd in protesting the admission of a black man, James Meredith, to the school.

Walker was awarded half a million dollars by a jury before the case was appealed to the Supreme Court.

James Meredith was the first black student admitted to the University of Mississippi. The Associated Press news service reported that a former army major general, Edwin Walker, led a crowd in protesting Meredith's admission. Walker sued for libel, but lost.

The Supreme Court reversed the judgment. It pointed out that a news service reporting fast-breaking news did not have time to check all the facts. Walker's position as a public figure influenced the Court's decision. Supreme Court Justice John Harlan said the AP story would not have seemed unlikely to people familiar with public statements previously made by Walker.

Generally, the press is allowed far greater freedom to criticize public figures than to criticize private citizens. In 1983 and 1984, *Hustler* magazine printed a satirical ad ridiculing political activist Rev. Jerry Falwell. The ad was, by the publisher's own admission, in bad taste, and grossly insulting. Falwell sued for damages.

Because *Hustler* had printed the words "Ad parody—not to be taken seriously" on the advertisement, the jury found that there was no libel. But they thought the ad was so outrageous that they awarded Falwell $200,000 for "emotional distress." This decision was upheld by an appeals court. The Supreme Court, however, unanimously overturned the verdict. As *Hustler* publisher Larry Flynt said, bad taste is not against the law. Satire aimed at

But political activist Rev. Jerry Falwell lost his suit against Hustler *magazine when the case reached the Supreme Court.*

public figures is a form of expression protected under the First Amendment.

The courts have continued to grant some protection to public figures who have been carelessly attacked in the press. In 1981, for example, entertainer Carol Burnett won a $1.6 million lawsuit against the *National Enquirer*, which published an article that claimed she had been drunk in a Washington restaurant.

Entertainer Carol Burnett won her lawsuit against the National Enquirer.

IV. RADIO AND TELEVISION

Radio and television are subject to more government control than are other forms of mass media. Unlike newspapers, books, and motion pictures, radio and television stations are licensed by the government. This is because Americans have decided that broadcast channels are a limited resource that

The control room of the WCCO-TV station in Minneapolis, MN. Television stations are subject to more regulation than newspapers or magazines.

belongs to everyone, a point of view that was upheld by the Supreme Court in 1969.

The first national legislation regarding broadcasting was passed in 1912. The Department of Commerce was assigned the task of issuing licenses and assigning wavelengths (air space) to private broadcasters, in order to keep civilian broadcasts from interfering with government wavelengths. The increasing number of stations, however, created such chaos over the airways that the radio industry asked the government for help. In response, Congress passed the Radio Act of 1927. The act established a five-person commission to regulate radio communications.

Federal authority over broadcasting was broadened in 1934 with the establishment of the Federal Communications Commission (FCC). The FCC was given the power to refuse to renew a radio license when a broadcaster was obviously disregarding the "public interest." The FCC has rarely used its regulating powers. Yet when it has, the Supreme Court has upheld its right to do so.

One well-known instance occurred

The FCC tries to make sure that radio stations broadcast programs that are in the public interest.

in 1978. Radio station WBAI-FM aired a 12-minute monologue from an album by comedian George Carlin. The routine, which was broadcast at 2:00 P.M., centered on the "seven filthy words" that were not allowed to be said over the air.

By the barest of margins, 5-4, the Supreme Court ruled that because of the public nature of the airwaves, the government could exercise much more authority over the content of radio programs than it could over the press. Not only could the government prohibit obscene material, but also material that was "patently offensive." In this case, the Court was particularly disturbed by the fact that an "adult" program was aired in the middle of the day, when children were likely to be listening.

Broadcasters currently operate under the Fairness Doctrine, introduced by the FCC in 1949. This policy states that broadcasters have a duty to provide a "reasonable

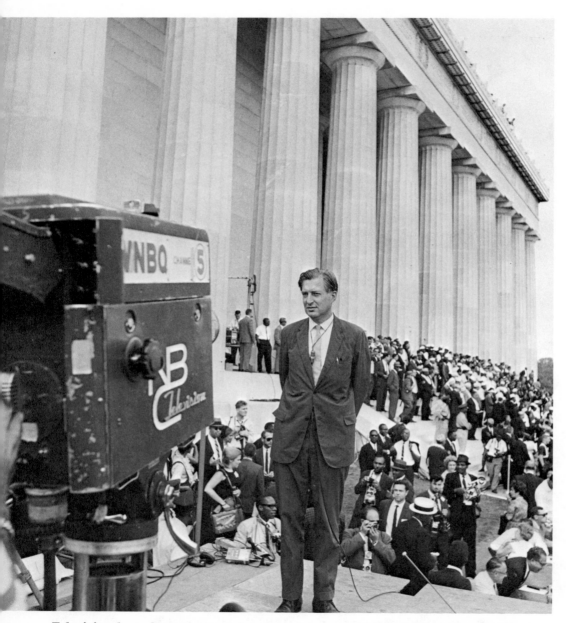

Television has always been an important source of information about public affairs. Here, a TV news crew covers the March on Washington in 1963. The march focused attention on the civil rights movement.

As a result of a case brought to the Supreme Court in 1968, cigarette advertising was banned from television. Cigarette ads can still be placed on billboards or in magazines or newspapers, however.

opportunity for the discussion of conflicting views on issues of public importance." One result of this ruling is that, in political campaigns, all candidates must be provided with equal time to present their views. This has caused confusion about the rights of very minor candidates.

In 1968 a young lawyer, John Banzhaf, used the Fairness Doctrine as the basis for a lawsuit aimed at cigarette advertising. Banzhaf claimed that television commercials for cigarettes promoted a controversial point of view on a major public health issue. According to the Fairness Doctrine, television stations should allow equal time for an oppos-

ing viewpoint. Congress responded to Banzhaf's argument by passing a law banning all radio and television advertising of cigarettes as of January 1, 1971.

Critics of government control over TV and radio note that there are now more than 12,000 radio stations and 1,100 TV stations in operation. Meanwhile, mergers and business failures have drastically reduced the number of daily newspapers. In light of these trends, some people question whether broadcast media are indeed more limited resources requiring greater government control than newspapers.

V. THE STUDENT PRESS

Should students who are working on a school newspaper be covered under the free press guarantees of the First Amendment? This issue has generated an increasing amount of debate. In 1987 the Student Press Law Center was notified of more than 500 cases of censorship of student publications.

In 1969 Supreme Court Justice Abe Fortas said that students do not "shed their constitutional rights to freedom of speech or expression at the schoolhouse gate."

In January of 1988, the Supreme Court again faced the issue. The test case arose out of Hazelwood East High School in Missouri, where Principal Robert Reynolds had cen-sored two pages of the May 13, 1983, issue of the school paper, the *Spectrum*. Reynolds thought that stories about teen pregnancy and divorce were inappropriate—particularly because the paper had not disguised the identities of those interviewed. The students who worked on the paper at the time took the matter to court, and eventually the case came before the Supreme Court.

In a 5-3 vote, the Supreme Court ruled against the students. Writing for the majority, Justice Byron White declared that "schools may impose reasonable restrictions on speech of students, teachers, and other members of the school community."

7
You Make the Decision

The following case will give you a chance to wrestle with many of the issues involved in freedom of the press. How would you decide if you were to judge this case? See how your decision stacks up against that of the New York jury that actually tried the case.

In 1983 *Time* magazine ran a cover story about the 1982 massacre of 700 Arabs in a refugee camp outside of Beirut, Lebanon. The murders were committed shortly after Lebanese president-elect Bashir Gemayel had been assassinated.

Time's article quoted from an official Israeli report on the incident which laid indirect blame for the killings on Israeli Defense Minister Ariel Sharon. Sharon interpreted

Ariel Sharon brought a lawsuit against Time Inc.

the article to mean that he had encouraged the murders. Outraged, he filed a $50 million lawsuit against Time Inc. in a New York court. After listening to the evidence, the following became apparent to the jury:

♦ the news report was false
♦ *Time* had acted negligently and carelessly in publishing the report
♦ *Time* was not aware that the story was false at the time of publication

Did the *Time* story defame Sharon? If so, was *Time* guilty of libel? Was Sharon entitled to collect damages?

What is your decision?

The jury that decided this case in 1985 said that since Ariel Sharon was a government official, the *Sullivan* rule applied to the case. In order to prove libel, Sharon needed to prove "actual malice." Although the jury strongly criticized *Time*'s reporting, the evidence did not show that the magazine had published the story with the knowledge that it was false.

8
Conclusion

Many other issues related to freedom of the press deserve consideration. Can the government deny reporters access to news stories, particularly in war zones? It has done so repeatedly. Does the press have a right to protect the identities of its news sources? The Supreme Court ruled in 1972 that it does not. Can police search newsrooms for evidence? The Supreme Court said in 1978 that they could. Two years later,

Since World War I, the Supreme Court has played a crucial role in interpreting the First Amendment and defining what freedom of the press means in the United States.

Questions and issues regarding freedom of the press are difficult to resolve. The First Amendment is continually being reinterpreted.

founding of the United States has generally been one of increasing respect for freedom. But in order for freedom to flourish, people must use that freedom responsibly. Some people will probably always abuse the privileges of freedom. Do we tolerate the abuses of the few to preserve freedom for the many? Or do we restrict everyone's freedom in order to punish the irresponsibility of a few? And if we do clamp down, who should decide what "abuse" is?

Issues concerning freedom versus responsibility are always difficult to resolve. Each generation must tackle these questions to determine the meaning and limits of freedom of the press in the United States.

Congress outlawed such searches. Does news coverage of a criminal case infringe upon the rights of the accused? The courts have acknowledged that it does, and they have ordered retrials or relocation of trials in cases where news reports may have influenced jurors. In these issues and all the others raised in this book, the key question is: What are the limits of freedom of the press in the United States?

A free press is vital to a democracy. The story of the press since the

For Further Reading

Adams, Julian. *Freedom and Ethics in the Press.* New York: Rosen Publishing Group, 1983.

Berger, Melvin. *Censorship.* New York: Franklin Watts, 1982.

Forer, Lois G. *A Chilling Effect: The Mounting Threat of Libel and Invasion of Privacy Actions to the First Amendment.* New York: W. W. Norton & Co., 1987.

Friendly, Fred W. *Minnesota Rag: The Dramatic Story of the Landmark Supreme Court Case That Gave New Meaning to Freedom of the Press.* New York: Random House, 1981.

Lieberman, Jethro. *Free Speech, Free Press, and the Law.* New York: Lothrop, Lee & Shepard, 1980.

Morris, Richard B. *The American Revolution.* Minneapolis, Minnesota: Lerner Publications Co., 1985.

———. *The Constitution.* Minneapolis, Minnesota: Lerner Publications Co., 1985.

———. *The Founding of the Republic.* Minneapolis, Minnesota: Lerner Publications Co., 1985.

Important Words

The terms listed below are defined on the indicated page:

Index

Acknowledgments

The photographs and illustrations in this book are reproduced through the courtesy of: Wendy Bell, pp. 2, 6; Library of Congress, pp. 8, 25, 30, 32 (bottom), 33, 35 (right), 40, 41, 53; Dow Jones & Company, Inc., pp. 9, 50; David Boe, p. 10; Independent Picture Service, pp. 11, 12, 20, 24, 26, 32 (top), 34, 35 (left), 36, 37, 42 (left), 44, 54, 67; Colonial Williamsburg, pp. 13, 18; The Louvre Museum, Paris, photo by Alinari, p. 14; Yale University, p. 16; State Historical Society of Wisconsin, p. 21; The New York Public Library, p. 23; The Virginia Museum of Fine Arts, Gift of Colonel and Mrs. Edgar W. Garbisch, 1950, p. 28; National Archives, p. 38; Quadrangle Books, p. 42 (right); Universal Press Syndicate, p. 46; Kerstin Coyle, pp. 47, 60, 72; Louisiana State Museum, p. 49; U.S. Army, p. 51; Department of Defense, p. 56; University of Georgia, p. 57; University of Mississippi, p. 58; Collector's Bookstore, p. 59 (left); Liberty Baptist College, p. 59 (right); Milton Blumenfeld, p. 61; NBC Photo, p. 62; Karen Sirvaitis, p. 63; Embassy of Israel, p. 65; Greg Helgeson, p. 68.